What Happens in the SPRING

Crocus blossoms push up through the snow.

by Kathleen Costello Beer

BOOKS FOR YOUNG EXPLORERS
NATIONAL GEOGRAPHIC SOCIETY

The cold winter is over, and a boy named Tracy
is outdoors looking for the first signs of spring.
He climbs over rocks and explores the countryside.
Tracy will spend many days discovering
the wonderful things that happen in the spring.

SNOWDROP

GROUNDHOG OR WOODCHUCK

PUSSY WILLOW
CATKINS

Tracy finds a white flower in the woods.
Then he sees a groundhog. It is awake
after sleeping underground all winter.
And the pussy willows are blooming!
Tracy can tell spring is on the way.

CANADA GEESE

LAMB AND EWE

Geese fly overhead.
They are going north
to their nesting places.
In the spring, many birds
return from the places where
they have been all winter.
A frisky lamb jumps and plays
near its mother.
Lambs and many other animals
are born in the spring.
A meadowlark sings and sings.
He is calling to his mate.
His song also tells the other birds
this part of the meadow is his.

EASTERN MEADOWLARK

BLOODROOT

EARTHWORM

*I*n a sunny spot, a spring flower opens its white petals.

Each day brings more sunlight. The days grow longer and longer, and the nights become shorter.

As the sun warms the earth, worms wiggle up through the soil. Ferns open as they begin to grow. The leaves of the skunk cabbage push up out of the ground. The mole knows it is spring. With long claws, it begins to dig its burrow and tunnels. Fur hides the mole's tiny eyes but not its long, pointed nose.

FIDDLEHEADS OF CINNAMON FERN

SKUNK CABBAGE

EASTERN MOLE

RED-WINGED BLACKBIRD

A stream becomes a busy place in the spring.
Tracy looks into the water. Among the rocks, he finds
a crayfish with long feelers and sharp claws.
He also sees a turtle crawling out of the mud,
where it has slept all winter.
A red-winged blackbird perches nearby.
At mating time, the male shows off
the red patches on his shoulders.

CRAYFISH

WOOD TURTLE

SPRING PEEPER

Tracy finds a tree frog
called a spring peeper.
It is so small that it can sit
on his thumb. The tiny frog
has a big voice. As it sings,
the skin under its chin
puffs up like a balloon.

9

The spotted salamander goes to a pond to mate
and lay its eggs in the water.
All the eggs are inside a blob of clear jelly.
Each dark egg becomes a tiny larva,
or baby salamander.
The larva lives in the water and breathes
through gills on the sides of its head.
Soon the salamander grows lungs
and can breathe air. Then it is ready
to leave the pond and live in moist places on land.

EGGS OF SPOTTED SALAMANDER

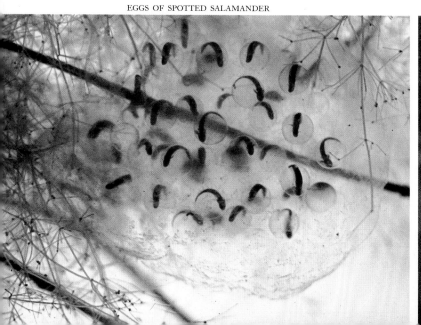

LARVA OF SPOTTED SALAMANDER

ADULT SPOTTED SALAMANDER

The spring rains and warm weather help the plants grow.
Tracy likes to feel the raindrops splash on his face.
The weather in the spring can change quickly.
The days can be so warm that trees begin to bloom.
Then the days may turn cold, and snow may fall on the flowers.
But soon it becomes warm again, and the snow melts quickly.

BUDS OF
AN APPLE TREE

ORCHARD GRASS

The rain
soaks the plants
and makes
deep
squishy
mud.

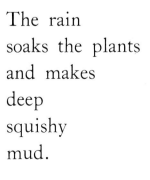

*W*ill Tracy fall off the fence? While Tracy tries to keep
his balance, his dog Killary rests. Behind them,
the trees that were bare all winter have flowers and leaves.
During the spring, trees go through several changes.
A small branch shows what happens to a maple tree.
First the flower buds swell up.
In a few days, the buds open into bright flowers.
Each female flower grows into red fruit.
Last, the leaf buds open into leaves. One day, Tracy sees
a butterfly land on the bark of a maple tree.

RED MAPLE BUDS

RED MAPLE FLOWER

RED MAPLE FRUIT

RED MAPLE LEAVES

COMMA BUTTERFLY

IRISH WOLFHOUND AND MAYAPPLES

BLUETS

*T*racy's dog sniffs the ground.
Killary smells something
among plants called mayapples.
What is Killary looking for?
It is not the flowers with purple petals.
It is the cottontail under a mayapple.
Killary is an Irish wolfhound.
She is very gentle and obeys Tracy.
He tells her not to harm the bunny.
Soon, Tracy finds four more bunnies.
He will put them gently
back into their nest.

COTTONTAIL RABBITS

PARULA WARBLER IN SOUTHERN BAYBERRY BUSH

Spring is a time of flowers and a nesting time for birds.
A sparrow rests among the white blossoms of an apple tree.
The little bird carries pieces of horsehair to line its nest.
A blue and yellow bird, called a warbler, sits in a bayberry bush.
This songbird usually stays high in trees, so it is hard to see.
In the forest, wild flowers bloom early,
before trees have leaves that block out the sun.

TROUT LILY OR DOGTOOTH VIOLET   HEPATICA

A mother bluebird sits on her nest.
She covers her eggs and keeps them warm.
When the eggs hatch,
the baby birds cannot stand or open their eyes.
They just chirp and wait for food.
The parents are busy catching insects for them to eat.
They eat and eat all day long, and they grow very fast.
In a few days, the little birds are covered
with soft feathers. And their eyes are open.

MALLARD HEN AND DRAKE

Mallards are ducks, and they can swim and fly.
The father duck is called a drake.
He has brighter feathers than the mother.
Her dull feathers help hide her
as she sits on her nest. Soon after her eggs hatch,
the ducklings walk and swim.
They waddle behind their mother into the water.

*I*nsects also hatch in the spring.

Many praying mantises wiggle out of their egg case all at once.

Tracy looks in the grass for other insects.

He watches two ladybugs on a plant. They are hunting for tiny aphids.

A ladybug catches one. A dragonfly has pulled itself out of its old skin.

Now the dragonfly has wings and is grown,

so it won't shed its skin anymore.

PRAYING MANTISES

LADYBUGS OR LADYBIRD BEETLES AND APHIDS

DRAGONFLY

*D*uring the winter,
this swallowtail butterfly was a pupa.
A pupa doesn't eat or move about.
It lives inside a shell, or case.
The pupa slowly turns into a butterfly
inside its case.
Do you see the bright wings through the case?
When spring comes, the case cracks open,
and the butterfly pulls itself out.
The butterfly began its life as an egg.
The tiny egg hatched into a caterpillar.
Later, the caterpillar changed into a pupa.

*T*racy huffs and puffs and blows the dandelion seeds away.
The white, fluffy seeds are so light they float through the air.
The seeds are formed as the yellow flowers wilt and die.
Wherever the seeds fall, new dandelions may grow.
Three baby skunks play in a field of dandelions.

STRIPED SKUNKS

*D*aisies, daisies, daisies. Spring has spread over the land, and summer is on the way. Animals are born or hatched. Flowers are in bloom. Bees buzz and fly from flower to flower. Trees are green. The days are long, and school is almost out. It is a happy, beautiful time. It is a time when children can go into the woods and fields to find the wonder and beauty of spring.

BUMBLEBEE ON DAISY FLEABANE

BLACK-EYED SUSAN

A butterfly lands on a flower.
It will sip the nectar
with its long tongue.
But first, it will taste
the sweet juice with its feet!

GREAT SPANGLED FRITILLARY ON SWEET VALERIAN

Published by The National Geographic Society
Robert E. Doyle, *President;* Melvin M. Payne, *Chairman of the Board;*
Gilbert M. Grosvenor, *Editor;* Melville Bell Grosvenor, *Editor Emeritus*

Prepared by
The Special Publications Division
Robert L. Breeden, *Editor*
Donald J. Crump, *Associate Editor*
Philip B. Silcott, *Senior Editor*
Cynthia Russ Ramsay, *Managing Editor*
Lucy E. Toland, *Researcher*
Wendy G. Rogers, *Communications Research Assistant*

Illustrations
Geraldine Linder, *Picture Editor*
Jody Bolt, *Art Director*
Suez Kehl, *Assistant Art Director*
Drayton Hawkins, *Design and Layout Assistant*
Cynthia E. Breeden, *Design Assistant*

Production and Printing
Robert W. Messer, *Production Manager*
George V. White, *Assistant Production Manager*
Raja D. Murshed, June L. Graham, Christine A. Roberts, *Production Assistants*
Debra A. Antonini, Jane H. Buxton, Mildred W. Forrest, Suzanne J. Jacobson, Amy E. Metcalfe, Cleo Petroff, Katheryn M. Slocum,
Suzanne Venino, *Staff Assistants*

Consultants
Dr. Glenn O. Blough, Peter L. Munroe, *Educational Consultants*
Edith K. Chasnov, *Reading Consultant*
Dr. Theodore R. Dudley, U. S. National Arboretum and the staff of the Smithsonian Institution, Washington, D. C., *Scientific Consultants*

Illustrations Credits
Herb Levart, National Audubon Society Collection/PR (1); James L. Stanfield, National Geographic Photographer (2-3, 3 top, 9 top, 12-13, 13 center and bottom, 22-23 bottom, 25 top, 28 top, 30 all, 31, 32); John Shaw, Bruce Coleman Inc. (3 center, 14 second in series); W. E. Ruth, Bruce Coleman Inc. (3 bottom); Bates Littlehales, National Geographic Photographer (4-5 top, 5 bottom, 8 top, 18 top, 22 top); Marie-Louise Brimberg (4 bottom, 16 bottom, 16-17 top); Walter Chandoha Photography (6 top); Wendy W. Cortesi, National Geographic Staff (6 left); R. Helstrom, Bruce Coleman Inc. (7 top left); Mary M. Thacher, National Audubon Society Collection/PR (7 top right); Dr. E. R. Degginger, Bruce Coleman Inc. (7 bottom); John Ballay, National Geographic Staff (8 bottom left); Ken Brate, National Audubon Society Collection/PR (8 bottom right); Larry West (9 bottom left, 14 bottom); D. R. Specker, Animals Animals (9 bottom right); F. E. Unverhau, Animals Animals (10 bottom left and right); Dr. Robert S. Simmons (11 top); Z. Leszczynski, Animals Animals (11 bottom); Roger Carr, Bruce Coleman Inc. (13 top, 14 first in series); Harry N. Darrow, Bruce Coleman Inc. (14 third in series); Grant Heilman (14 fourth in series); William R. Curtsinger (15); Charles E. Mohr, National Audubon Society Collection/PR (17 bottom left); Jack Dermid (17 bottom right); Guy Starling, National Geographic Staff (18 bottom left); Virginia Findley (18 bottom right); Thase Daniel (19); Lawrence Zeleny (20 top); Michael L. Smith (20 bottom left and right, 21); Leonard Lee Rue III, National Audubon Society Collection/PR (22 center left); Laura Riley, Bruce Coleman Inc. (22 center right); J. R. Simon, National Audubon Society Collection/PR (23 top); Stan Wayman, National Audubon Society Collection/PR (24); Robert F. Sisson, National Geographic Natural Science Photographer (25 center left and right); Alvin E. Staffan, National Audubon Society Collection/PR (25 bottom); David T. Overcash, Bruce Coleman Inc. (26 all, 27); Stouffer Productions Ltd., Bruce Coleman Inc. (28 bottom); Jane Burton, Bruce Coleman Inc. (29)

Cover Photograph: James L. Stanfield, National Geographic Photographer
Endpaper Painting: Ned M. Seidler, National Geographic Staff Artist

Library of Congress ℂℙ data
Beer, Kathleen Costello.   What Happens in the Spring.   (Books for young explorers)
SUMMARY: Describes the changes in plants and animals in the spring.
1. Spring — Juvenile literature. {1. Spring} I. Title. II. Series.
QH81.B413   574   77-76970   ISBN 0-87044-242-2